Neighbors Near and Far

by Barbara L. Luciano

PEARSON

Scott
Foresman

Editorial Offices: Glenview, Illinois • Parsippany, New Jersey • New York, New York
Sales Offices: Needham, Massachusetts • Duluth, Georgia • Glenview, Illinois
Coppell, Texas • Sacramento, California • Mesa, Arizona

A community is a special place.
People live in communities.

Large communities can be in the city.

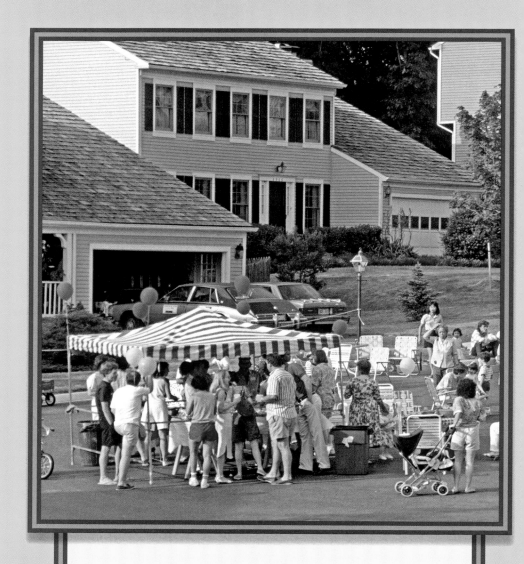

A suburb has homes and families.
It is near the city.

Small communities can be in the country. They are far from the city.

Communities can be the same.
They all have signs, homes,
and streets.

What makes your community a special place to live?

Glossary

city community where lots of people live

community where people live

country community where few people live

large big

sign something that gives people information

small little

store place to buy things

street place to drive

suburb community with homes and stores